[illegible] CALL ME BOB!

Patti Monro

illustrated by Rosemary Allen

GINN

GINN

1996 UK edition published by Ginn and Company Limited
Prebendal House, Parson's Fee, Aylesbury, Bucks HP20 2QY
ISBN 0 602 27006 5

Printed in Hong Kong by Dah Hua Printing Press Co., Ltd.

Reprinted in 1997

CONTENTS

CHAPTER ONE

Wet birthday

The day I became a teenager was the day of the big flood.

Times were hard. My birthday present was covered with brown paper and tied with string. I didn't know what was inside it.

Twiggy, our dog, didn't know what was inside it either. She sat and waited for me to open the present.

"Open it, Bobby," Mum said. She sat and waited too. "Open the present. It'll knock you over!"

I opened the present slowly. All eyes were on me. Oh, no! It knocked me over all right! Inside were yellow socks and a yellow jacket.

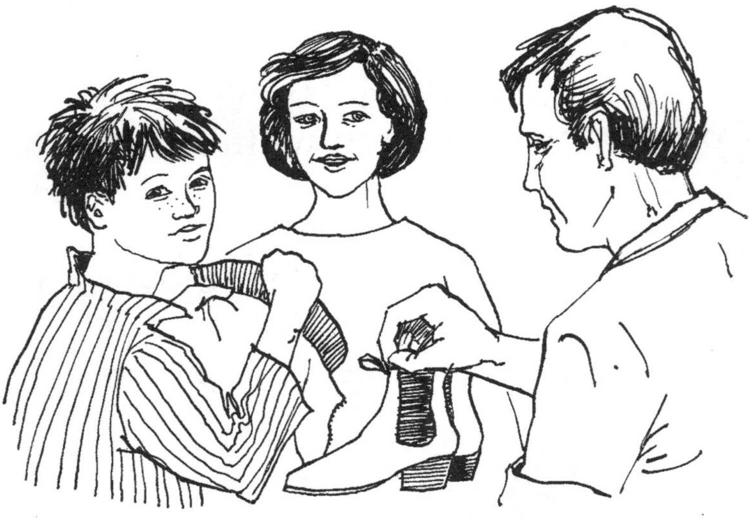

"Yellow's the latest — good colour for safety!" said Mum.

The style of the jacket was cool; a zip front and lots of zip pockets. But the colour — oh, no!

"Trendy gear, eh, sonny?" said Dad, as he handed me a pair of new boots. "Happy birthday!"

I felt I had turned three years old, not thirteen. I had hoped for a skateboard.

I tried to look pleased. "Thanks," I said to them.

I tried not to grit my teeth with annoyance. It really bugged me to be called by baby names and to get such dumb presents.

"Stop calling me Bob-by and son-ny," I said to myself. "Why can't they call me Bob and son?"

CHAPTER TWO

No mates nearby

Our family was living on a farm at the time. Dad was the caretaker for a few months, so Mum and I had moved out to the farmhouse to be with him.

On and off we had lived in a nearby town that few people had heard of. I went to high school in this town. I had lots of mates there. But we had to go where Dad could get work.

Our family consisted of just the three of us, Mum, Dad and me. I had no brothers or sisters. Now, out on the farm, I had no mates either. It wasn't much fun.

The farm had a river running through it with low-lying flats on the far side. This river looked more like a creek to me. But Dad said it was named as a river on the map. I looked it up in an atlas. He was right. There it was, marked with a long blue line going west to join the Darling River.

CHAPTER THREE

Where was all the fun?

The day I became a teenager was just an ordinary sort of day. It was school holidays. There was no school bus to rush for. Yes, it had been raining, raining quite a lot.

"Good for winter feed," said Dad. "The farmers can plant their crops, too."

I put on the socks to please Mum. Yellow! What a dumb colour!

"I'm glad none of my mates can see me," I thought to myself.

Mum made me do some jobs inside the house even though it was my birthday.

"I have to work on *my* birthday," Mum said. "Why shouldn't you?" I wished I was back in town with my mates.

"Go *on*, Bobby," she went on. "Stop dreaming. Get the jobs over and done with."

"Don't call me Bobby. I'm not a pre-schooler. Haven't you noticed?"

The words slipped out. I didn't mean to let her see how bad I was feeling. I was having a rotten birthday. Where was all the fun?

"Try saying, 'Please call me Bob'. It's more polite."

I grinned. "Please, Mum-my, call me Bob." This was said in my three-year-old voice.

CHAPTER FOUR

Phone for Dad!

So I did do my jobs inside. Then I went outside to find Dad.

But boring, boring birthday! Where was all the action? If I was in town, my mates would come round right now for some fun. They would give me thirteen punches on the arm. Then we would go down town to the pin-ball machines. Later, we would go to the edge of town and watch older boys on trail bikes. We would have a heap of fun.

On the farm, there was a motorbike outside the shed near the house. It was just like a trail bike, only it was used to muster sheep. I knew how to ride it. In fact, I had ridden it a few times; only when Dad wasn't looking. Fat chance of riding it today with Mum and Dad around!

"Bobby, Bobby!" Mum yelled from the house. "Phone call for Dad. Get him quickly."

"OK. But please call me Bob!" I yelled back.

CHAPTER FIVE

Where are all the sheep?

Dad hurried out of the house. "Sonny! Would you like a job, an outside job? You can ride that motorbike. I know you can."

I waited to see what the job was. I said nothing.

"Mr Warner, next door, has just rung. He says there's a flood warning for the river. We'll have to move some sheep from the low flats in the Far Paddock. The sheep are trapped there. They'll drown if we don't move them to higher ground.

We'll have to use the flood boat to reach them from this side of the river. We'll get Twiggy to give us a hand."

Twiggy sat up and listened too. She looked as pleased as I felt when Dad told me what to do.

"Take the bike. Before we can do anything about saving the sheep, I need to know two things. How quickly is that water rising? Where are all the sheep?"

He waved a hand towards the river and went on. "Follow the river upstream from this high side. Check the water levels as you go. Look out for any mobs of sheep in the Far Paddock. I need to know where to go to rescue them."

He reached the shed. "I'll move the tractor and plough from the Low Paddock while you're gone. Mum's ringing neighbours to check on river levels upstream!"

Twiggy hopped on the bike with me. Her front paws were on the handle-bars. Away we went.

CHAPTER SIX

Ready! Set!

"Yes, you *will* have to move the sheep today," I told Dad when Twiggy and I returned. "The river has flooded the Far Paddock at the upstream end. The water's still rising. Most of the sheep are safe on high ground. We'll need the boat to move the rest."

"Right! I'll take you and the dog. We'll leave as soon as we can."

We were ready to go in ten minutes. Mum gave us some tucker for smoko.

Dad put oars, spare fuel and the outboard motor in the boat. Then we lifted it onto the truck. I put life-jackets in at the last minute.

"Here's your new jacket, Bobby. Take it with you. It'll be cold later." This was from Mum, of course.

"Please call me Bob. I'm a teenager, don't forget." I waved goodbye.

"I'll have roast lamb and mint sauce for your birthday dinner when you get back."

"I'd rather have Pizza Special," I said to myself.

CHAPTER SEVEN

Go!

There was a chilly nip in the air as we set off to save the sheep. Winter was on the way. It had stopped raining.

Twiggy was beside me in the front of the truck. Her nose was pointing out of the window into the wind. She panted with joy. Someone was enjoying my birthday.

"Tell me, sonny," Dad asked. "Tell me again just where those floodbound sheep were — and how many. We mustn't lose any."

"They're up at the eastern end of the Far Paddock. I saw a small mob there. A couple of dozen or more, I'd say."

"That sounds right. We must save them all, eh, Twiggy?"

Twiggy put her head inside and panted at me. We reached the river and drove along the high bank upstream to find the sheep.

Within half an hour of leaving home, we were off in the boat to save the sheep. Twiggy put her nose into the wind, sniffing.

Suddenly, she started yelping.

"There they are, sonny!" Dad shouted.

"Don't call me sonny," I yelled.

The sheep were standing still with floodwater almost up to their hooves. Our job was to move them to the safety of higher ground.

CHAPTER EIGHT

Twiggy to the rescue

"How do we do it Dad? There are too many to fit in the boat."

Dad laughed and looked at Twiggy. She panted with joy. She leapt out of the boat into the water.

We jumped out of the boat too. I was wearing my new boots. I was glad Mum couldn't see me.

The sheep wouldn't move. We shouted, the dog yapped and we tried to push them to higher ground, but they wouldn't move. Dumb animals, sheep!

"Well, son! What next?"

I looked at the sheep and looked at the boat. Thirty or so sheep and one boat.

Twiggy looked at Dad and looked at me. She put her front paws on the side of the boat. She knew what to do.

"Six sheep to a boat-load, I reckon," said Dad. "That's five or so trips." He looked at the afternoon sun in the west." "We'll be lucky to do it before dark."

CHAPTER NINE

My good idea

So Dad and I lifted six sheep into the boat for the first rescue trip. Twiggy made sure they didn't jump out.

"There's not much spare room," said Dad.

"Talking of room, Dad, if I stayed behind here you could move more sheep. You could put one more sheep in the boat instead of me. It could save you one trip."

Dad looked at me. "I don't like that idea much. It's safer to stay together."

Then he looked again at the sun in the west.

"OK, son. It *is* a good idea. We must move them before nightfall."

CHAPTER TEN

Up the tree

So, I was left behind with the mob of stranded sheep. I found a tall gum tree to sit in. It was like a lookout for a ship at sea. I looked down at the murky floodwaters rising below me. I looked at the sheep huddled together. I looked at Dad disappearing out of sight in the boat.

What if Dad didn't find me again? What if all tall gum trees looked the same above the water? What would I do? I might be up the tree all night. I might starve. I ate a tiny bit of Mum's tucker for smoko. I thought of my mates in town. I thought of the skateboard I wanted. I felt so alone.

Suddenly, I realised I wasn't alone. I was sharing the tree with other animals escaping from the flood.

There were grubs and bugs on the branch with me and higher up there were drenched birds sitting quietly.

I started to climb towards a higher branch. Dad could see me more easily up there. I went carefully up the wet tree trunk.

Then, horror! I put my hand on a hidden snake. I slipped in fright. I grabbed a small branch. It broke and I bumped and bounced through the tree into the floodwater. Help!

I was scratched and bruised but the water broke my fall.

"Come on! Get up and give me a hand!" Dad was back.

"Dad, I fell out of the tree! I'm hurt! I put my hand on a snake! It might have bitten me!"

"You look OK to me. You'd know if you'd been bitten. Here, grab this sheep will you, sonny."

"*Don't* call me son-ny. I'm a teenager now!"

"Well act like one, will you. Grab the next sheep. NOW! We're running out of daylight fast." Dad sounded mad.

I felt mad.

So, each time Dad returned I helped to load more sheep. Each time Dad left, I sat up the tree on my own. It was cold. I was wet. Everything hurt. I had the jitters.

My mates in the town seemed a very long way off. I began to look forward to Mum's roast lamb and mint sauce. All I could see here was wet lamb and mud sauce as the rising floodwater swept by.

The sheep stood up to their knees in water now. The sun sank lower in the west.

CHAPTER ELEVEN

Soggy singing

Twiggy stayed with me when Dad went on the last trip to save the sheep. She sat in my arms up the tree. My yellow jacket was torn. My yellow socks and new boots were soggy. The dog was wet. I thought of roast lamb; Twiggy would enjoy the bone inside it. The sun had gone down. It was dark. We were just plain scared.

I started to sing. Then I couldn't hear the suck and swirl of the floodwater about me.

"Nice song, son!" said Dad. "I heard your voice and saw your yellow jacket. Ready for the trip home?"

"Am I ever!"

Twiggy wagged her tail.

We jumped into the boat with Dad.

CHAPTER TWELVE

Down the river

"It's too far upstream to the truck. The boat won't make it back there. We'll go downstream with the current. Put on your lifejacket, son. Take off your boots, like me. Boots make you sink faster if you're swimming for your life."

The night was pitch black. We headed for the river across the flooded flats. The boat bumped into logs and stumps that were hidden underwater. Twiggy's nose was pointing into the wind, her front paws on the edge of the boat.

"Keep that dog down in the boat. She'll get tossed out!" yelled Dad.

I made the dog lie down under a seat in the boat.

We reached the river. We were in deep water; it flowed fast. Dad steered. I was the lookout.

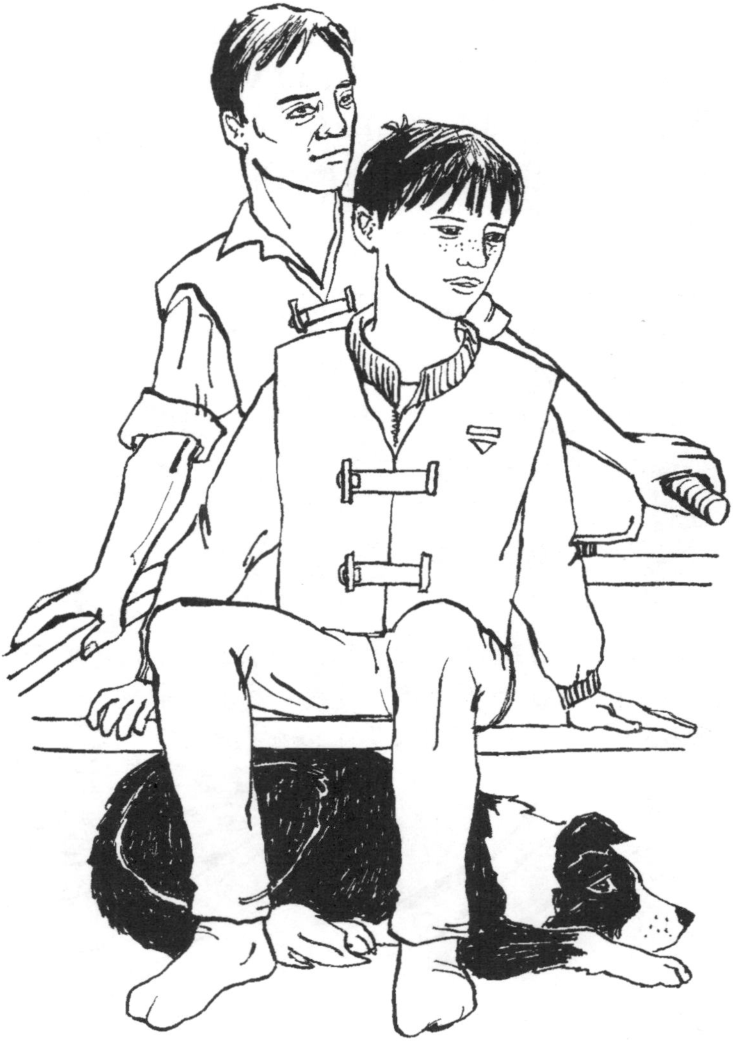

"Sharp bend to the left! Barbed-wire fence to the right, Dad!"

We were jolted this way and that.

"Look out, Dad . . .!"

Too late! A wall of water overtook us. There was nothing we could do. The boat was washed over a huge log. It spun around and tipped us into the water.

Dad and I were in the river, swept along by the flood. We were swimming for our lives. It was pitch black. Where was Twiggy?

"Swim for the high side … if you can … look out for logs racing down … don't get a knock on the head!"

"Lucky … I remembered … the lifejackets!" I gasped.

"Lucky … we took off … our boots!" Dad puffed.

We struggled across the torrent to the high side of the river. We climbed the bank and collapsed at the top.

"Let's have a rest, Dad" I pleaded.

"We'll get our breath!" he agreed.

And in the silence that followed, we heard a well-known yelp.

"Twiggy!" we both shouted.

We couldn't believe it! The boat had swirled across and was bumping on the bank below. There was Twiggy, safe and sound, lying under the seat.

"Lucky the boat's unsinkable," we both rejoiced.

CHAPTER THIRTEEN

A teenager at last!

"Ready for the hike home?"

"Are we ever!"

Twiggy pointed her nose towards home and led the way. Dad and I followed in our socks. My birthday boots were gone. We were drenched. We were dog-tired.

I just put one foot in front of the other and plodded on. There was no road to follow. We just followed the dog over rocks and logs and through puddles and mud. We wore holes in our socks and got burrs in our feet.

"Burrs are no softer under water!" Dad grumbled.

"Rocks are no smoother, either!" I mumbled.

I had forgotten about food, friends and family. It seemed a long, long way.

At last, we saw the lights of the house ahead. We started to sing. Twiggy beat us home. My mother came out to meet us.

"Is that you men out there?" Mum called into the darkness.

Then with a loud cheer, my school mates rushed out of the house. What a shock!

"Happy birthday!" they yelled.

They shoved a Pizza Special into one hand and a new skateboard into the other.

"Happy birthday, mate!" they yelled again and gave me thirteen punches on the arm.

"A great day's work, son," said Dad.
"Well done, Bob," said Mum.
Twiggy said nothing, because she was busy eating the roast lamb, bone and all.